Grass Bug

written by Anne Giulieri

photography by Ned Meldrum

Look at my *grass* bug.
It is very *hairy*!

A grass bug is fun to make.
You can make one too!

To make a grass bug, you will need:

a spoon

cotton balls

grass seeds

a plastic lid
from a jar

black paper

two big googly eyes

a jug of water

scissors

strong glue
and a brush

5

To make your grass bug,
get the lid.
The lid goes like this.

To make the legs
get the black paper.
Cut out 6 legs.

Then glue the legs
on top of the lid.

You can *bend* the legs like this.

The lid and legs go like this. Then *cotton balls* go inside the lid.

9

Then get the two big *googly eyes.* They go on the cotton balls like this.

Then get a *spoon*
to help you with the *seeds*.
The seeds go on top of
the cotton balls like this.

You need a little bit of *water*.
The water goes
into the lid like this.

MAY

MON	TUE	WED	THU	FRI	SAT	SUN
		1	2	3	4	5
6	7	8	9	10	11	12
13	14	15	16	17	18	19
20	21	22	23	24	25	26
27	28	29	30	31		

Look at the bug.
It is not hairy.

Look at the bug.

It is getting a little bit of hair.

Your bug will need a little bit of water in the day.

13

Look at the bug again.

It looks very hairy!

MAY

MON	TUE	WED	THU	FRI	SAT	SUN
		1	2	3	4	~~5~~
~~6~~	~~7~~	~~8~~	~~9~~	~~10~~	~~11~~	~~12~~
~~13~~	~~14~~	~~15~~	~~16~~	~~17~~	~~18~~	~~19~~
~~20~~	~~21~~	~~22~~	~~23~~	~~24~~	~~25~~	(26)
27	28	29	30	31		

Oh, no!

The grass bug is gone!

Can you find it hiding in the grass?

Picture Glossary

bend

grass

spoon

cotton balls

hairy

water

googly eyes

seeds